How Much of Man is Natural?

Two versions of the international prize-winning essay

Neil Paul Cummins

Cranmore Publications

A catalogue record for this book is available from the British Library

ISBN: 978-1-907962-20-2

Published by Cranmore Publications

Reading, England

For Paul

Contents

Preface

In 2008 the Spinoza-Gesellschaft ran an international prize essay competition. There was a set title for the contest: *How much of man is natural?* This is a topic about which I thought I had some interesting things to say so I entered the competition. I was fortunate enough to win.

This book contains the winning entry in its original form. Three years have passed since I wrote this original paper and in that time my views have become a little more refined. On reading the essay again I also found some of the passages to be unclear or to be 'claiming a bit too much'. For these reasons I have created a modified version of the winning essay. I hope that this modified essay is clearer and a little less speculative (even 'fruity') in places than the original.

Introduction

There is little more to say by means of an introduction; the essays will largely introduce themselves. However, I should make it clear that in the title of the essay the word 'man' is being used to refer to the human species as a whole. The topic of the essay is not whether there are different degrees of naturalness between 'man' and 'woman'. So, one can read the title as "How much of the human species is natural?" if one so wishes. Or even: "How much of a human is natural?"

I claim in the essays that humans are wholly and entirely natural. This doesn't mean that there aren't differences (and potentially important differences) between the 'non-human natural universe' and the 'human natural universe'. Furthermore, it doesn't mean that there aren't important differences between 'men' and 'women'. Indeed, it seems plausible to me that 'women' in some fundamental sense could be much more similar to the 'non-human natural universe' than 'men'. This perhaps sounds a bit cryptic, and it is another story, for another time (you might have already read my books "Is the Human Species Special?" and/or "The purpose of the Environmental Crisis"). For now, our concern is simply the naturalness of all humans.

Essay One

The Winning Essay

The definition of natural is 'present in or produced by nature'. Is it not obvious to anyone who thinks about the question of 'how much of man is natural' that man has been *produced by* nature, and that every fibre of his being and existence is *present in* nature? Surely, a more appropriate question would be: "How could man possibly doubt that he is completely natural?"

In a trivial sense man, as a creator of words, can create a word such as 'natural', and define it in such a way that it excludes man. The word 'natural' can be opposed to either 'artificial' or 'supernatural'. However, interestingly, the word 'artificial' is defined as 'made by humans; produced rather than natural'. This definition does not refer to man *himself*, rather the word 'artificial' is itself an arbitrary construct, a word of use in human communication because it enables the *productive activities of man* to be referred to. There is no notion in the word 'artificial' that man himself is not natural. Furthermore, there is no implication that in the world itself there is a fundamental division in nature that the word 'artificial' refers to. It is simply of use to man to have a word that labels the results of his productive activities.

The notion of 'human production' is actually a deeply problematic one. If one gives the matter no real thought then the distinction between the 'natural' and the 'artificial' seems to be obvious, but deep reflection reveals otherwise. It is obviously the case that before the human species evolved nothing was artificial. It also seems obvious that objects such as the sun and the planet Jupiter are not artificial. But when we focus on the Earth then it is hard to identify anything that is truly natural. Let us consider a tree that is growing in a rainforest, and a tree that is produced in a human factory. One would be tempted to call the former 'natural' and the latter a 'produced artefact'. However, when one learns that the rainforest tree has the particular attributes

13

that it has because humans soaked the surrounding ground with nutrients and breathed additional carbon dioxide into the vicinity of the tree, then one might have to concede that the tree is an artefact.

Similarly, a human-constructed wigwam-shaped structure composed of branches would be a 'produced artefact', but a single branch lying on the ground under a tree would be considered 'natural'. Even if a human steps on the branch and breaks it the branch would still be considered to be 'natural'. But there is no difference in kind between modifying a branch by stepping on it, and moving several branches into a wigwam structure. At a larger scale human activities have modified the climate and atmosphere of the entire planet thereby making the concept of the 'natural', as opposed to the 'artificial', largely redundant when it comes to the Earth. It is worth noting that it is also possible to argue that even the sun and Jupiter are 'artificial' because many people hold that the act of human observation itself affects what is observed, meaning that everything in the universe that is referred to by man has been 'created' by man. In its contemporary guise this view asserts that observation collapses quantum wavefunctions from a superposition of possible states into particular concrete states. So, there really is no meaningful distinction *in reality itself* between the 'artificial' and the 'natural'.

The word 'supernatural' is defined as: 'of or relating to existence outside the natural world'. It has to be questionable whether this word has any meaning whatsoever – surely all that exists is the natural world – *nothing* exists outside it. The word 'supernatural' is also used to refer to 'a power that seems to violate or go beyond natural forces' and 'of or relating to the miraculous'. These descriptions are instructive because they imply that man uses the word 'supernatural' to refer to those parts of the world around him that he cannot comprehend. So, in the past a total eclipse of the sun would have been referred to as a supernatural event, a miracle. But now such an event is simply considered to be a natural occurrence. This means that the word 'supernatural' delineates man's understanding of how the world works from how it actually works. It doesn't imply that in reality parts of the world are necessarily not natural. The word 'supernatural' should surely be thought of in an epistemological sense rather than an ontological sense.

So, the word 'artificial' simply refers to the 'productive' activities of man in the world, and the word 'supernatural' can be thought of as delineating the limits of man's understanding of the world. These words are perfectly compatible with the belief that man is wholly natural, and the belief that all that exists is the natural world. In fact, if one denies this and argues that man is not wholly natural, then the complex and intricate way in which the activities of man modifies man's surroundings leads to the inextricable problem of delineating what is natural

17

from what is not natural. On facing this problem one would seem forced to conclude that the entire biosphere of the Earth is not natural. It is surely more sensible to conclude that the whole of the Earth is natural, and that *the word 'artificial' refers to things that, whilst produced by man, are still natural.*

Nevertheless, the very fact that man can doubt whether he is natural is clearly of interest. To understand the existence of this doubt we need to deconstruct the word 'natural'. Natural has been defined as: 'present in or produced by nature'. The word 'nature' itself has not yet been defined, but is contemporarily defined as: 'the material world and its phenomena'. This definition of nature sheds light on why man could possibly doubt that he is completely natural. It is the contemporary conception of nature as the 'material world' that causes man to doubt whether he is 'natural' because man himself doesn't seem to be composed of 'mere matter'.

In the face of this doubt there are two 'naturalistic' options. It could be argued that 'mere matter' has the ability to *produce* entities such as man that have states of qualitative feeling and self-awareness. Alternatively, it could be argued that man's knowledge of 'nature' is still at a primitive level and that the label 'material world' is deeply misleading; it could be the case that all of nature has states of qualitative feeling. Either way, man, in reality, is still wholly natural. The alternative – that man is not natural, but 'ontologically supernatural' – creates an unwarranted division in reality. The real issue is the epistemological one of our ignorance about the fundamental nature of 'nature'. I take that it would be nonsensical to assert that man could be *partially* natural; that man could be dissected into both natural parts and non-natural parts.

Most of the above analysis relies on the definition of words – definitions that can help explain why man might not consider himself to be natural, *given* the definition of natural. However, there is a much deeper issue. There will be a great number of contemporary humans who are totally unaware of the definition of natural, and who have not considered how they relate to nature. It is surely the case that the vast majority (if not all) of these humans consider themselves to be opposed to the surrounding world in some fundamental way. In other words, it could be a fundamental characteristic of what it is to be human to conceive of oneself as opposed to the surrounding world. The most likely basis of this opposition is the existence of self-awareness. So, even if man is totally natural, his self-awareness could lead to the perception that he is divided from the rest of the world in some fundamental way, and so is not 'natural'.

Therefore, there are two distinct issues. Firstly, given that the word natural means 'present in or produced by the material world and its phenomena', what could it possibly mean for man to be 'not natural'? Secondly, if man is wholly natural why does he doubt his 'naturalness'? Why does he consider himself to be opposed to the surrounding world? These two questions are obviously closely interrelated because it is the belief in an opposition between man himself and the surrounding world which leads to the conceptualizing of that world as 'mere matter'. If the belief in an opposition didn't exist then the natural world itself would, no doubt, not be conceptualized as 'mere matter'. Rather, it would be conceptualized in such a way that the attributes of man and world are tightly coupled.

Man's perception of the natural world

It goes without saying that man's perception of the natural world has varied immensely through time, and that it also varies between different cultures in the contemporary epoch. It is the dominant 'western view' of the natural world which I will focus on here. It is this view that establishes a particularly sharp division between man and world, a division that is so deep that man's naturalness can be seriously doubted. According to the 'western view' the natural world is a clockwork mechanism the activities of which have been increasingly accurately predicted through science. The operations of the non-living world are thoroughly deterministic and

23

are wholly devoid of qualitative feeling, intentionality and awareness. In contrast, man has 'free will' to
act in ways which cannot be predicted by science,
and has qualitative feeling, awareness and intentionality. Some people distinguish man from the
'natural' world through asserting that man has
attributes that can be referred to as 'consciousness'
or 'mind' – I won't use these terms as they are not
needed and are a source of great confusion.

Of course, there are those who live in the 'west'
who don't subscribe to the 'western view'. Some
people hold that the entire natural world has
intentionality, or qualitative feeling, or awareness,
or that quantum physics shows that the entire
natural world has freedom. Others argue that man

himself doesn't have free will – it is simply an illusion. What is one to make of the claims of these people who oppose the 'western view'? The issues raised are very deep any many seem to be unanswerable. Who could say whether there are states of aboutness or directionality ('physical intentionality') when atoms interact to form molecules? Who could say whether these interactions themselves entail qualitative feeling? Who could say whether there is any kind of awareness present in these interactions? Who could say whether these interactions actually result from free will? And who could possibly know if every thought that they have ever had is determined, and in theory predictable before they had it?

I take it that nobody has adequate answers to these questions. Therefore, the question needs to be asked as to why the 'western view' always sides with the 'oppositions' – the answers to the questions which lead to an opposition between man and world. This 'siding' clearly says nothing about the natural world *itself* – all it reveals is the way in which man perceives himself in relation to that world.

I obviously do not claim to have answers to the above questions. However, I do not see any good reason why, given that man was produced by nature, that there should be a great chasm between the attributes of man and world. Surely, if man has qualitative feeling, then it has to be very likely that the world that produced him has qualitative feeling.

Surely, if man has free will, then it has to be very likely that the world that produced him has free will. Contrarily, if all the thoughts and actions of man are determined, then it has to be very likely that the activities of the world that produced him are also determined. This doesn't mean that man cannot have unique attributes, just as a human eye has attributes that a human finger lacks. It is possible that the high-level of reasoning and thinking that occurs in the area of space-time that is a human is a unique attribute of man. It is also possible that this results in an awareness in man that is lacking in the (rest of the) natural world. But, just as the body of man is pervaded by unique attributes, and just as the attributes of mercury are very different to those of helium, uniqueness doesn't entail a fundamental division in reality. It is surely the case that the vast majority of the attributes of man are shared by the entire natural world. Whilst every phenomena in the natural world (including man) also has some kind of uniqueness when analyzed in detail.

It could be argued that the question: "How much of man is natural?" should be replaced with the question: "How many of the attributes of man are not present in the non-human world?" At a first glance this question would seem to provide some kind of an answer to the former question. If it was concluded that man has a plethora of attributes that are not present in the non-human world then this would seem to imply that a large proportion of man is not natural. Whilst, contrarily, if it was concluded that there are hardly any 'unique' human attributes this would indicate that man is very largely natural. However, it is clear that the latter question cannot provide any kind of answer to the former question. Whilst the latter question is a valid question to ask it is comparable to asking the question: "How many of the attributes of mercury are not present in the non-mercury world?" There clearly are attributes of mercury that are not present in the non-mercury world, because it is the presence of these attributes that makes mercury mercury. But it would be nonsensical to conclude from this that the question: "How much of mercury is natural?" is a sensible question to ask. It is simply the case that within the natural world there are differences in the attributes of the various phenomena that exist; some phenomena will closely resemble others, and some will not.

It is time to consider the place of non-human animals. We have seen that 'natural' is defined as 'present in or produced by the material world and its phenomena', and is conceptually opposed to both 'artificial' and 'supernatural'. Given these 'oppositions' what are we to make of the 'naturalness' of other animals. We know that all living things modify their surrounding environment, and that many species of animals are very human-like in their activities. For example, chimpanzees are tool-users, beavers construct dams, and birds construct nests. These activities and modifications of the surrounding world by non-human animals are clearly not 'artificial', because artificial is defined as 'made by humans; produced rather than natural'. They are surely also not 'supernatural', which is defined as: 'of or relating to existence outside the natural world'. These activities are surely wholly natural.

I take it that it would be nonsensical to describe non-human animals themselves, a dam constructed by a beaver, or the tools created by chimpanzees, as anything other than wholly 'natural'. But I also take it that it would be woefully inadequate to describe beavers and chimpanzees as 'mere matter'. It is surely the case that at the very least qualitative feeling states exist in beavers and chimpanzees; many would argue that they can have self-awareness as well. In other words, there are close links between the attributes of humans and those of beavers and chimpanzees. But, it has been accepted that beavers and chimpanzees, and their activities, are wholly natural. They are wholly produced by and present in the material world; so, they are either 'mere matter' or the result of the interactions of 'mere matter'. This means that, just like in humans, a certain amount of tension is created in that beavers and chimpanzees are both 'natural' and 'more than mere matter' at the same time. This means that a naturalistic account requires either endowing 'mere matter' with the power to generate qualitative feeling, or accepting that all 'matter' has qualitative feeling.

This tension gets to the heart of the issue of the relation between man and the 'natural world'. In fact, other animals are an 'intermediary' between man and phenomena such as mercury. It seems easy to assert that mercury is both wholly natural and 'mere matter'. But when it comes to animals such as the chimpanzee, whilst it is easy to assert that it is wholly natural, it also seems to be correct to assert that it is 'more than mere matter'. This tension gets continued into the realm of man, because man is also surely 'more than mere matter' whilst also being natural. It is this tension which leads to the conclusion that maybe man is not wholly 'natural', as the 'natural' is fundamentally 'mere matter'. But if we accept this conclusion then we surely also have to accept that some non-human animals are also not wholly 'natural'. This is surely unacceptable.

What are the other alternatives? If the similarities between man and certain species of non-human animals are accepted, which they surely should be, then it has to be accepted that if these non-human animals and their activities are wholly natural, then so is man and his activities. If it is accepted that qualitative feeling states exist in these non-human animals then we have to conclude that either 'mere matter' has the power to generate qualitative feeling in these species, or that all 'matter' has qualitative feeling. However, we do not know which of these two scenarios is correct. Given this, it would surely be sensible to change our conceptualization and definition of 'natural' by ridding it of the notion of the 'material' world. In other words, we should initially accept our ignorance about the fundamental nature of reality, and then we should conclude that the word 'material' is vacuous. This means that we can then define 'natural' as: 'present in or produced by the world and its phenomena'. This definition quite helpfully rids us of the notion of the 'super-natural'. It also leaves open the possibility that the entire world is pervaded by states of qualitative feeling. If this conceptualization became the dominant view of the man-nature relationship, rather than the 'western view', then surely man would consider himself to be wholly natural. In the present epoch man largely doubts his 'naturalness'.

Why does man doubt his 'naturalness'?

It could be argued to be a sign of the primitive intelligence level of man that he can on the one hand talk of the evolution of all species from a common ancestor and the Big Bang, and yet, on the other hand, he can doubt his 'naturalness'. Alternatively, one could argue that it is not really a matter of intelligence, but rather that man is simply that part of nature which *of necessity* considers itself to be not natural. In other words, in the form of man, nature has produced a kind of 'reflective mirror' which enables nature to do things that are impossible without such a mirror. A useful analogy is the hairdresser, who is capable of creating the perfect haircut for her clients without a mirror, but who can only produce a dreadful mess on her own hair without the aid of a mirror. If the hairdresser produces a mirror she will gain the ability to perfectly cut her own hair, just as nature clearly gains abilities through producing man.

If this is right; if man has unique abilities in nature due to not considering himself to be natural, then this means that it is inevitable that man will doubt his naturalness. To be man *is* to consider oneself to be not natural; to be opposed to the surrounding world; to be alienated from the rest of nature. So, this means that it is inevitable that man will doubt his 'naturalness'. It could be argued that this doubt is an inevitable side-effect of self-awareness itself. However, I would argue that self-awareness is a necessary but not a sufficient condition for the generation of such doubt. It is possible that some of the areas of space-time that we call 'non-human animals' have self-awareness without such doubt. It is also possible to imagine a future in which man doesn't doubt his 'naturalness'. However, in this future world the areas of self-aware space-time that today we label 'man' would be so different that they surely wouldn't even use the word 'man' to refer to themselves, or 'nature' to refer to the 'material' world and its products. They would just drop the arbitrary labels and accept their 'oneness'.

Concluding remarks

I have argued that man is completely and utterly natural in every fibre of his being. The word 'artificial' is simply a label that is used in human communication to refer to the productive activities of man in the world. The word 'supernatural' simply delineates man's understanding of how the world works from how it actually works.

It has also been argued that some species of non-human animals are sufficiently similar to man that if man isn't wholly natural then this implies that that these non-human species are also not wholly natural. Furthermore, it has been asserted that the notion of the 'semi-natural' is nonsensical. This is a logical point and also derives from the futility of attempting to divide the phenomena of the Earth up into the 'natural' and the 'artificial', or the 'natural' and the 'supernatural'. The inextricability of this division forces one to accept that everything is natural.

Once it is accepted that everything is wholly natural one has to accept that the attributes of man and world are tightly coupled. Given that man has qualitative feeling, awareness and intentionality one has to *wonder in ignorance* whether these attributes exist throughout nature. This ignorance means that we should redefine nature as: 'present in or produced by the world and its phenomena'. This definition makes the notion of the 'supernatural' redundant as everything that exists, exists in the world.

It has been proposed that a more perplexing question than: "How much of man is natural?" is, "How could man possibly doubt that he is completely natural?" I have argued that man is that part of nature which *of necessity* considers itself to be not natural. It is this perception, this doubt, which gives man his unique position in nature. If this doubt were to cease then although the biological areas of space-time that we call 'man' would still exist, these areas would be so different to those that exist today that using the name 'man' to refer to them would be inappropriate. 'Man' and 'doubt' are inextricably linked. Nevertheless, man is wholly and utterly 'natural'.

Essay Two

The Modified Essay

The definition of natural is 'present in or produced by nature'. Is it not obvious to anyone who thinks about the question of 'how much of man is natural' that man has been *produced by* nature, and that every fibre of his being and existence is *present in* nature? Surely, a more appropriate question would be: "How could man possibly doubt that he is completely natural?"

In a trivial sense man, as a creator of words, can create a word such as 'natural', and define it in such a way that it excludes man. The word 'natural' can be opposed to *either* 'artificial' *or* 'supernatural'. However, interestingly, the word 'artificial' is defined as 'made by humans; produced rather than natural'. This definition does not refer to man *himself;* rather the word 'artificial' is itself an arbitrary construct, a word of use in human communication because it enables the *productive activities of man* to be referred to. There is no notion in the word 'artificial' that man himself is not natural. Furthermore, there is no implication that in the world itself there is a fundamental division in nature that the word 'artificial' refers to. It is simply of use to man to have a word that labels the results of his productive activities.

The notion of 'human production' is actually a deeply problematic one. If one gives the matter no real thought then the distinction between the 'natural' and the 'artificial' seems to be obvious, but reflection reveals otherwise. It is obviously the case that before the human species evolved nothing was artificial. It also seems obvious that objects such as the Sun and the planet Jupiter are not artificial. But when we focus on the Earth, then it is hard to identify anything that is truly natural. Let us consider a tree that is growing in a rainforest, and a tree that is produced in a human factory. One would be tempted to call the former 'natural' and the latter a 'produced artefact'. However, when one learns that the rainforest tree has the particular attributes that

45

it has because humans soaked the surrounding ground with nutrients and breathed additional carbon dioxide into the vicinity of the tree, then one might have to concede that the tree is an artefact.

Similarly, a human-constructed wigwam-shaped structure composed of branches would be a 'produced artefact', but a single branch lying on the ground under a tree would be considered 'natural'. Even if a human steps on the branch and breaks it the branch would still be considered 'natural'. But there is no difference in kind between modifying a branch by stepping on it, and moving several branches into a wigwam structure. At a larger scale human activities have modified the climate and atmosphere of the entire planet thereby making the concept of the 'natural', as opposed to the 'artificial', largely redundant when it comes to the biosphere of the Earth. So, there is no meaningful distinction *in reality itself* between the 'artificial' and the 'natural'.

The word 'supernatural' is defined as: 'of or relating to existence outside the natural world'. It has to be questionable whether this word has any meaning whatsoever – surely all that exists is the natural world – *nothing* exists outside it. The word 'supernatural' is also used to refer to 'a power that seems to violate or go beyond natural forces', and also 'of or relating to the miraculous'. These descriptions are instructive because they imply that man uses the word 'supernatural' to refer to those parts of the universe around him that he cannot comprehend. So, in the past a total eclipse of the sun would have been referred to as a supernatural event, a miracle. But now such an event is simply considered to be a natural occurrence. This means that the word 'supernatural' delineates man's *understanding* of how the universe works from how it *actually* works; it doesn't imply that in reality parts of the universe are not natural. A complete description of the universe would include solely 'natural' phenomena; there wouldn't be any 'supernatural' phenomena.

So, the word 'artificial' simply refers to the productive activities of man in the world, and the word 'supernatural' can be thought of as delineating the limits of man's understanding of the world. These terms are perfectly compatible with the belief that man is wholly natural, and the belief that all that exists is the natural world. Indeed, if one denies this and asserts that the world, and the Earth, contains natural parts and non-natural parts then one faces a seemingly inextricable problem. One has to try to untangle the complex and intricate way in which the activities of man have modified man's surroundings in order to separate what is natural from what is not natural. If one attempted to do this then one would surely conclude that the entire biosphere of the Earth is *not* natural. It is surely more sensible to conclude that the whole of the Earth is natural, and that *the word 'artificial' refers to things that, whilst produced by man, are still natural.* Alternatively, if one really believes that *the world itself* is split into the natural and the supernatural, then one has to specify exactly what these supernatural entities are. History suggests that there are no such entities because as understanding increases the 'supernatural' gets reclassified as natural.

Nevertheless, the very fact that man can doubt whether he is natural is clearly of interest. To understand the existence of this doubt we need to deconstruct the word 'natural'. Natural has been defined as: 'present in or produced by nature'. The word 'nature' itself has not yet been defined, but is contemporarily defined as: 'the material world and its phenomena'. This definition of nature sheds light on why man could possibly doubt that he is completely natural. It is the contemporary *conception* of nature as the 'material world' that causes man to doubt whether he is 'natural' because man himself doesn't seem to be composed of 'mere matter'.

In the face of this doubt there are two 'naturalistic' options. Firstly, one could hold that the term 'mere matter' is an accurate description of much of the world, but that man is not made of 'mere matter', and therefore that 'mere matter' has the ability to *produce* entities such as man which are not made of 'mere matter'. Secondly, one could hold that the term 'mere matter' is vacuous – there are no parts of the world that fit the term. In other words, one can hold that man's knowledge of 'nature' is still at a primitive level and that the label 'material world' is deeply misleading; it could be the case that all of nature has states analogous to those in man. Both of these options are 'naturalistic' options; both entail that man *is* wholly natural. However, if one's beliefs put one into the first group then it is much more likely that one will consider oneself to *not* be natural.

Most of the above analysis relies on the definition of words – definitions that can help explain why man might not consider himself to be natural, *given* the definition of natural. However, there is a much deeper issue as the definitions themselves are clearly expressions of man's pre-existing conceptual framework. The real issue is why man's conceptual framework in the current epoch is such that he defines nature as the 'material world and its phenomena'. Why do most contemporary humans consider themselves to be opposed to the surrounding world in some fundamental way? Could it be that it is a fundamental characteristic of what it is to be human to conceive of oneself as opposed to the surrounding world?

There are clearly two distinct issues. Firstly, given that the word natural means 'present in or produced by the material world and its phenomena', what could it possibly mean for man to be 'not natural'? Secondly, if man is wholly natural why does he doubt his 'naturalness'? Why does he consider himself to be opposed to the surrounding world? These two questions are obviously closely interrelated because it is the belief in an opposition between man and the surrounding world which leads to the conceptualizing of that world as 'mere matter'. If the belief in an opposition didn't exist then the natural world itself would, no doubt, not be conceptualized as 'mere matter'. Rather, it would be conceptualized in such a way that the attributes of man and world are tightly coupled.

Man's conception of the natural world

It goes without saying that man's conception of the natural world has varied immensely through time, and that it also varies between different cultures in the contemporary epoch. It is the dominant contemporary 'western view' of the natural world which I will focus on here. This view establishes a particularly sharp division between man and world, a division that is so deep that man's naturalness can be seriously doubted. According to the 'western view' the natural world is a clockwork mechanism the activities of which have been increasingly accurately predicted through science. The operations of the non-living world, and much of the living world, are conceived of as thoroughly deterministic and are wholly devoid of qualitative feeling, intentionality and awareness. In contrast, man has 'free will' to act in ways which cannot be predicted by science, and has qualitative feeling, awareness and intentionality.

Of course, there are those who live in the 'west' who don't subscribe to the 'western view'. Some people hold that the entire natural world has intentionality, or qualitative feeling, or awareness, or that quantum physics shows that the entire natural world has freedom. Others argue that man himself doesn't have free will – it is simply an illusion. What is one to make of the claims of these people who oppose the 'western view'? The issues raised are very deep any many seem to be unanswerable. Who could say whether states of aboutness/intentionality exist when atoms interact to form molecules? Who could say whether these interactions themselves entail qualitative feeling? Who could say whether there is any kind of awareness present in these interactions? Who could say whether these interactions actually result from free will? And who could possibly know if every thought that they have ever had is determined, and in theory predictable before they had it?

I take it that no-one has adequate answers to these questions. Therefore, the question needs to be asked as to why the 'western view' always sides with the 'oppositions' – the answers to the questions which lead to an opposition between man and world. This 'siding' clearly says nothing about the natural world *itself* – all it reveals is the way in which man perceives himself in relation to that world.

I obviously do not claim to have answers to the above questions. However, I do not see any good reason why, given that man was produced by nature, that there should be a great chasm between the attributes of man and world. This doesn't mean that man cannot have unique attributes, just as a human eye has attributes that a human finger lacks. It is possible that the high-level of thought that occurs in a human is a unique attribute of man. But, just as the body of man is pervaded by unique attributes, and just as the attributes of mercury are very different to those of helium, uniqueness doesn't entail a fundamental division in reality. It is surely the case that the vast majority of the attributes of man are shared by the entire natural world; whilst every phenomenon in the natural world (including man) also have some kind of uniqueness when analyzed in detail.

It could be argued that the question: "How much of man is natural?" should be replaced with the question: "How many of the attributes of man are not present in the non-human world?" At a first glance this question would seem to provide some kind of an answer to the former question. If it was concluded that man has a plethora of attributes that are not present in the non-human world then this would seem to imply that a large proportion of man is not natural. Whilst, contrarily, if it was concluded that there are hardly any 'unique' human attributes this would indicate that man is very largely natural. However, it is clear that the latter question cannot provide any kind of answer to the former question. Whilst the latter question is a valid question to ask it is comparable to asking the question: "How many of the attributes of mercury are not present in the non-mercury world?" There clearly are attributes of mercury that are not present in the non-mercury world, because it is the presence of these attributes that makes mercury mercury. But it would be nonsensical to conclude from this that the question: "How much of mercury is natural?" is a sensible question to ask. It is simply the case that within the natural world there are differences in the attributes of the various phenomena that exist; some phenomena will closely resemble others, and some will not.

It is time to consider the place of non-human animals. We have seen that 'natural' is defined as 'present in or produced by the material world and its phenomena', and is conceptually opposed to both 'artificial' and 'supernatural'. Given these 'oppositions' what are we to make of the 'naturalness' of other animals. We know that all living things modify their surrounding environment, and that many species of animals are very human-like in their activities. For example, chimpanzees are tool-users, beavers construct dams, and birds construct nests. These activities and modifications of the surrounding world by non-human animals are clearly not 'artificial', because artificial is defined as 'made by humans; produced rather than natural'. They are surely also not 'supernatural', which is defined as: 'of or relating to existence outside the natural world'. These activities are surely wholly natural.

I take it that it would be indefensible to describe non-human animals themselves, or their constructions, as anything other than wholly 'natural'. But I also take it that it would be woefully inadequate to describe beavers and chimpanzees as 'mere matter'; there are close links between the attributes of humans and the attributes of these non-human animals. But, it has been accepted that beavers and chimpanzees, and their activities, are wholly 'natural'. This means that they are wholly produced by or present in the material world; they are either 'mere matter' or the result of the interactions of 'mere matter'. So, as with humans, there is a clear tension here – beavers and chimpanzees are both 'natural' *and* they are 'more than mere matter' at the same time.

This tension gets to the heart of the issue of the relation between man and the 'natural world'. In fact, other animals are an 'intermediary' between man and phenomena such as mercury. It seems easy to assert that mercury is both wholly natural and 'mere matter'. But when it comes to an animal such as a chimpanzee, whilst it is easy to assert that it is wholly natural, it also seems to be correct to assert that it is 'more than mere matter'. This tension gets continued into the realm of man, because man is also surely 'more than mere matter'. It is this tension which leads to the conclusion that maybe man is not wholly 'natural' because the 'natural' is fundamentally 'mere matter'. But if we accept this conclusion then we surely also have to accept that some non-human animals are also not wholly 'natural'. This is surely unacceptable.

What is the alternative? If the similarities between man and certain species of non-human animals are accepted, which they surely should be, then it has to be accepted that if these non-human animals and their activities are wholly natural, then so is man and his activities. Furthermore, we should change our conceptualization and definition of 'natural' by ridding it of the notion of the 'material' world. In other words, we should initially accept our ignorance about the fundamental nature of reality, and then we should conclude that the word 'material' is vacuous. This means that we can then define 'natural' as: 'present in or produced by the world and its phenomena'. This definition quite helpfully rids us of the notion of the 'supernatural'. It also leaves open the possibility that there is a tight coupling between the attributes of man and world. If this conceptualization became the dominant view of the man-nature relationship, rather than the 'western view', then surely man would consider himself to be wholly natural. In the present epoch man doubts his 'naturalness'.

How Much of Man is Natural?

Why does man doubt his 'naturalness'?

It is slightly paradoxical that man can on the one hand talk of the evolution of all species from a common ancestor and the Big Bang, and yet, on the other hand, he can doubt his 'naturalness'. Perhaps this is so because man is that part of nature which *of necessity* considers itself to be not natural. In other words, in the form of man, nature has produced a kind of 'reflective mirror' which enables nature to do things that are impossible without such a mirror. A useful analogy is the hairdresser, who is capable of creating the perfect haircut for her clients without a mirror, but who can only produce a dreadful mess on her own hair without the aid of a mirror. If the hairdresser produces a mirror she will gain the ability to perfectly cut her own hair, just as nature clearly gains abilities through producing man.

If this is right – if man has unique abilities in nature due to not considering himself to be natural – then this means that it is inevitable that man will doubt his naturalness. To be man *is* to consider oneself to not be natural; to be opposed to the surrounding world; to be alienated from the rest of nature. On this view it is inevitable that man will doubt his 'naturalness'.

Concluding remarks

I have argued that man is completely and utterly natural in every fibre of his being. The word 'artificial' is simply a label that is used in human communication to refer to the productive activities of man in the world. The word 'supernatural' simply delineates man's understanding of the world from the way the world actually is.

I have claimed that some species of non-human animals are sufficiently similar to man that if man isn't wholly natural then this implies that these non-human species are also not wholly natural. I have also claimed that it would be futile to attempt to divide the phenomena of the Earth up into the 'natural' and the 'artificial'; the inextricability of the 'artificial'/'natural' division forces one to accept that everything is natural.

I have proposed that a more perplexing question than: "How much of man is natural?" is, "How could man possibly doubt that he is completely natural?" I have suggested that man is that part of nature which inevitably comes to consider itself to not be natural. It is this belief, this doubt, which gives man his unique position in nature. Man and doubt are inextricably linked. Nevertheless, man is wholly and utterly natural.

Other books by the author:

Is the Human Species Special? : Why human-induced global warming could be in the interests of life

Should I be a Vegetarian? : A personal reflection on meat-eating, vegetarianism and veganism

The Purpose of the Environmental Crisis : *A Reinterpretation of Hölderlin's Philosophy*

www.ingramcontent.com/pod-product-compliance
Lightning Source LLC
Chambersburg PA
CBHW050606280326
41933CB00011B/2001